1991

THE SELF

The Aquinas Lecture, 1988

THE SELF

Under the auspices of the
Wisconsin-Alpha Chapter of Phi Sigma Tau

by

ANTHONY KENNY

Marquette University Press
Milwaukee
1988

Library of Congress Catalogue Number: 88-60191

Copyright 1988
Marquette University Press

ISBN 0-87462-155-0

Prefatory

The Wisconsin-Alpha Chapter of Phi Sigma Tau, the National Honor Society for Philosophy at Marquette University, each year invites a scholar to deliver a lecture in honor of St. Thomas Aquinas.

The 1988 Aquinas Lecture, *The Self*, was delivered in the Todd Wehr Chemistry Building on Sunday, March 27, 1988, by Anthony Kenny.

Anthony Kenny was born on March 16, 1931 and was educated at St. Francis Xavier's College, Liverpool, and then at St. Joseph's College, Upholland. In 1949 he went to the Venerable English College in Rome where he took the licentiate in philosophy in 1952 and the licentiate in theology in 1956. He was ordained to the Roman Catholic priesthood in 1955 and laicised in 1963. From 1964 to 1978 he was a fellow of Balliol College, Oxford and twice senior tutor. He has been Master of Balliol College since 1978.

He was elected to the British Academy in 1974 and the Royal Society of Edinburgh in 1979. He has been the Wilde Lecturer in Natural Religion at Oxford (1969-72) and Gifford Lecturer at the University of Edinburgh (1972-73). From

1980 to 1983 he held the Speaker's Lectureship in Biblical Studies at Oxford and was the Stanton Lecturer at Cambridge. He was Visiting Professor at the University of Minnesota in 1982. In 1982 he received an honorary degree from Bristol, and he will become Warden of Rhodes House, Oxford, in October, 1989.

Professor Kenny's publications include: *Action, Emotion and Will* (1963), *Descartes* (1968), *The Five Ways* (1969), *Wittgenstein* (1973), *The Anatomy of the Soul* (1974), *Will, Freedom and Power* (1975), *Aristotelian Ethics* and *Freewill and Responsibility* (1978), *Aristotle's Theory of the Will* and *The God of the Philosophers* (1979), *Aquinas* (1980), *The Computation of Style* (1982), *Faith and Reason* and *Thomas More* (1983), *The Legacy of Wittgenstein* (1984), *A Path from Rome*, *The Logic of Deterrence*, *The Ivory Tower*, *Wyclif*, *A Stylometric Study of the New Testament*, and *The Road to Hillsborough* (1986), *Reason and Religion* and *The Heritage of Wisdom* (1987).

To Professor Kenny's distinguished list of publications, Phi Sigma Tau is pleased to add: *The Self.*

THE SELF

My topic this evening is the philosophical concept of the self. It is a topic which needs no introduction or apology. What can be more intimate or important to each of us than our self? The poet Thomas Traherne wrote

A secret self I had enclos'd within
That was not bounded with my clothes or skin.

The self of which Traherne speaks is what is most personal and private to each of us. Most people never see beyond our clothes; a few intimates have seen the uncovered nakedness of our skins; but no human being other than myself has seen my self. Other people--each of us may feel--can know me in a sense, but what they can know of me is only what is exterior; however familiar they may be with me, however hard they may try, they can never reach to the real self within.

The philosophical concept of the self has been given dramatic expression by another poet, Arthur Hugh Clough. In a powerful though incomplete verse drama,

The Mystery of the Fall, Clough identifies the self as the locus of the primeval sin of Adam. He makes Adam claim for his innermost ego nothing less than divine status.

> Though tortured in the crucible I lie,
> Myself my own experiment, yet still
> I, or a something that is I indeed,
> A living, central, and more inmost I
> Within the scales of mere exterior me's
> I -- seem eternal, O thou God, as Thou.

Clough was an extraordinarily introspective person, with a morbid fear of the slightest insincerity or affectation. It is no accident that he should be able to express so vividly the thought that one's public selves are a carapace to be sloughed off.

It is significant, however, that he places this thought in the mouth of the sinful Adam. Other writers have seen the self as the locus not of sin but of sanctity. Robert Bolt, in his play *The Man for All Seasons* makes the motivating force which takes Thomas More to martyrdom his hero's "adamantine sense of self." More, says Bolt, was a man who knew how far he would yield to love and to fear, but who became rigorous and unyielding when at last "he was asked to retreat from that final area where he located himself." More died rather than swear a false oath, because, as he says in the play, "When a man takes an oath he's holding his own self in his own hands. Like water; and if he opens his fingers then, he needn't hope to find himself again."[1]

But of course it is not poets and dramatists, but philosophers who are most given to talking about the self. The Oxford English Dictionary lists a special philosophical sense of the word "self" which it defines as follows:

> That which in a person is really and intrinsically *he* (in contradistinction to what is adventitious); the ego (often identified with the soul or mind as opposed to the body); a permanent subject of successive and varying states of consciousness.

It is the purpose of this lecture to claim that the self of the philosophers is a mythical entity, and so likewise is the self of the poets and dramatists to the extent to which it is modelled on the philosophers' myth.

At one level, "the self" is a piece of philosopher's nonsense consisting in a misunderstanding of the reflexive pronoun. To ask what kind of substance my *self* is is like asking what the characteristic of *ownness* is which my own property has in addition to being mine. When, outside philosophy, I talk about myself, I am simply talking about the human being, Anthony Kenny, and my self is nothing other than myself. It is a philosophical muddle to allow the space which differentiates "my self" from "myself" to generate the illusion of a mysterious metaphysical entity distinct from, but obscurely linked to, the human being who is talking to you.

The grammatical error which is the essence of the theory of the self is in a manner obvious when it is pointed out. But it is an error which is by no means easy to correct; that is to say, it is by no means easy to give an accurate account of the logic, or deep grammar, of the words "I" and "myself." It will not do, for instance, to say simply that "I" is the word each of us uses to refer to himself, a pronoun which when it occurs in sentences is synonymous with the name of the utterer of the sentence.

This is not difficult to show. Julius Caesar, in his *Commentaries*, regularly described his own actions in the third person, using the name "Caesar." (In our own time General De Gaulle sometimes affected a similar manner of speaking). There might be a language, call it Caesarian, in which there were no first person pronouns, and in which everyone talked about themselves by using their own names. We may ask whether everything we can say in English can be said in Caesarian. The answer is clearly no. If Caesar wishes to deny that he is Caesar (perhaps wishing to test the perspicacity of a new petitioner at court, like the Dauphin faced with Joan of Arc), then in English he can tell the lie, "I am not Caesar." In Caesarian no similar option is open to him. "Caesar is not Caesar" will not do the trick. Nor will "the person who is speaking to you is not Caesar." For in Caesarian that sentence in Caesar's mouth is equivalent to the English sentence, "The person who is speaking to you is not I."

The truth is that "I" does not refer to the person who utters it in the way in which a proper name refers to its bearer. Neither does "myself." This does not mean that these words refer to something else, say my self. In fact, neither "I" nor "myself" is a referring expression at all. It is, of course, true that the truth-value of sentences uttered by X containing the words "I" and "myself" will be determined by what is the case about X. But this fact about the truth conditions of such sentences does not determine the meaning of the items within the sentence. Elsewhere, following a lead given by Professor G. E. M. Anscombe, I have tried to sketch the grammar of these first person expressions.[2]

In this lecture I do not intend to pursue further the grammatical issues I explored earlier. For though belief in a self is in one sense a grammatical error, it is a deep error and one which is not generated by mistaken grammar alone. The error has a number of different roots, and these need to be pulled up if the weed is to be eradicated. We may concentrate in the present lecture on two of the roots: the epistemological root and the psychological root. The myth of the self takes different forms in accordance with the root from which it takes its growth.

The epistemological root of the notion of the self is Cartesian scepticism. Descartes, in his *Meditations*, convinces himself that he can doubt whether the world exists, and whether he has a body. He then goes on to argue, "I can doubt whether I have a body; but I cannot doubt whether I exist; for what is this I which is doubting?" The "I" must refer to something of which his body is no part, and hence to something which is no more than a part of the human being Descartes. The Cartesian ego is a substance whose essence is pure thought, the mind or *res cogitans*. This is the self in the second of the philosophical senses identified by the O.E.D. "the ego identified with the soul or mind as opposed to the body."

Attempts to give content to the notion of a Cartesian ego run into two intractable problems. The first problem concerns the relation of that ego to the body from which it has been distinguished. The second concerns the relation between the underlying mental substance and its successive conscious states. I shall not develop either problem in this lecture, but simply record my opinion that the two problems prevent any coherent content being given to the notion of *res cogitans*.

Scholastics prior to Descartes had, of course, distinguished between mind and body. They spoke more commonly of "soul and body," and regarded the mind as one aspect or faculty of the soul. Descartes was uncomfortable with the word "soul" because in the mouths of Aristotelians who believed that animals and even plants had souls, the word was not mentalistic enough. What was new in Descartes was not the use of "mind" rather than "soul" so much as the identification of the person with the mind rather than with the body-soul composite.

When Descartes asked himself, "What am I?" he gave the answer, "A mind." A scholastic would have answered, "I am not my soul any more than I am my body; I am a person, but no part of me is a person. My body is a part of myself, and my soul is a part of myself. When I die, even if my soul leaves my body, I shall no longer exist, and I shall not exist again unless there is a resurrection of the body."

The epistemological route to the notion of the self takes us to a self which is much more circumscribed than the scholastic notion of the soul or of the intellectual mind. For the Cartesian ego is the substratum of those states of mind about which doubt is impossible. But there are many states of the intellect, as that was conceived by the scholastics, which are not exempt from doubt and where the first person is in no position of infallible authority.

The intellect is the faculty whereby I understand, judge, know, believe. It is far from being the case that whenever I think I understand, judge, know, or believe something, I do in fact understand, judge, know and believe that thing. An undergraduate may believe he understands the ontological argument; it may not take an examiner more than a few moments to convince him that he does not. We used to think we could make judgements about the class of all classes that are not members of themselves; it took the genius of Russell to convince us that no such judgement could be made. Each of us could list many things we once believed ourselves to know which in the end turned out to be false and therefore unknowable. And often, in connection with religious or political beliefs, we say to ourselves, "Is that something I really believe -- or am I only pretending?"

If Descartes wishes to say that we are infallible about the contents of our own minds, the most he can claim with plausibility is that we know what we are thinking at a given moment. No one, he may say, is better placed than yourself to answer the question, "A penny for your thoughts?"--and while in answer to that question you may lie, you cannot be mistaken. Surely I am infallible about what I am visualising in my mind's eye, or saying to myself in my head! That is something which I *know*, and which *only I* know, or at least only I *really* know, since others will have to take my word for it and they cannot be sure I am not deceiving them.

Somebody with a scholastic training might reply that in that case what Descartes is identifying himself with is his imagination, not his intellect. The images of inner vision, and the words of inner monologue are *phantasmata*, exercises of the fancy rather than of the intellectual mind. Of course, the intellect and the imagination are linked: these phantasms have the significance they have because of the intellectual capacity of the imaginer. If I do not know French I cannot talk to myself in French any more than I can talk to you in French.

Even with regard to the immediate contents of consciousness the authority of the first person is limited. When what is in question is the occurrence of words in the imagination, the first person may have the last word about what sound he imagined, but he does not have the last word about the significance of those sounds. Suppose that someone suffers from the vulgar delusion that "refute" means "contradict," and says to himself, *sotto voce*, "I have thoroughly refuted those slurs on my integrity." We won't challenge his claim to have used the word "refute" to himself, but we will claim to know better than he what the word really means. And in a sense we will claim to know better than he what thought really went through his head: what he was thinking was not that he had successfully refuted the slurs, but that he had vigorously contradicted them.

Among the activities which the medieval tradition ascribed to the intellect was the activity of doubting. Here, surely, one might think, Cartesian infallibility applies. We may be mistaken about what we know or understand, but surely we know when we are doubting! But even this is wrong. The death-blow to the whole Cartesian programme was given when Wittgenstein made us realize that even the words used to give private expression to Cartesian doubt would not have any sense in a world which contained nothing but a Cartesian ego.

The Cartesian ego is one version of the myth of the self: the version which grows from an epistemological root. A different and richer version of the myth is to be found in empiricist philosophy after Locke. This grows from a psychological root rather than from an epistemological root: it derives from a particular picture of the nature of introspection.

From the point of view of medieval philosophy the Lockean self no less than the Cartesian ego takes its rise from a confusion between the intellect and the imagination. However, it owes its particular character to an erroneous picture of the imagination which it must be admitted was common to medieval scholastics as well as to seventeenth-century empiricists.

Scholastic philosophers, followed by Locke, conceived of the imagination as an inner sense. That is to say, they thought that when I conjure up a mental image, my relation to the image in my mind is similar to my relation to a picture I look at in an art gallery, except that in the one case I am looking at an inner image, and in the other case I am looking at an outer picture. Similarly, when I talk to myself *sotto voce*, I hear with my inner ear words which I produce with my private voice, just as when I hold a conversation with you I hear with my outer ear words which you produce with your public voice.

The notion of an inner sense is a misleading one, whether in the scholastics or in the empiricists. It exaggerates the superficial similarities between sensation and imagination, and conceals the profound conceptual differences between the two. Sense faculties -- such as the sense of sight, hearing, taste, smell, and touch -- are faculties for discriminating between public data which different subjects, depending on their cirumstances, may be in better or worse positions to observe. The objects of imagination are created, not discovered; there is no such thing as gradual approximation to the optimal discernment of them. There can be no such thing as control by one observer on the acuteness of another's

discrimination between phantasms. Imagination is not a peculiar kind of sensation;
it is ordinary sensation phantasized. Because imagination is phantasized sensation,
and because sensation is essentially discrimination, to imagine is to phantasize discrimination. But to imagine that one is discriminating is not the same thing as to dis-
criminate between images.

The objects of imagination are
misdescribed when imagination is conceived as an inner sense. But much more
seriously, the notion of an inner sense
misrepresents the subject of imagination
too. The self, as misconceived in the
empiricist tradition, is essentially the subject of inner sensation. The self is the eye
of inner vision, the ear of inner hearing; or
rather, it is the mythical possessor of both
inner eye and inner ear and whatever other
inner organs of sensation may be
phantasized.

Hence, if the whole notion of inner
sense is misconceived, then not only the
objects of imagination are misunderstood
when regarded as inner sense-data, but so
also, more importantly, there is a misunderstanding underlying the idea that there

is an inner subject of sensation, the self of empiricist tradition.

If I am right, the self of modern philosophical theory is a chimaera begotten of empiricist error. But, notoriously, thoroughgoing empiricism has also had a problem in making room for the self. Empiricism teaches that nothing is real except what can be discovered by the senses, whether inner or outer. The self, as inner subject, can clearly not be discovered by the outer senses, which perceive only the visible, audible, tangible exterior of things. But can it be discovered by the inner sense either? It is well known that Hume, after the most diligent investigation, failed to locate the self.

> When I enter most intimately into what I call *myself*, I always stumble on some particular perception or other, of heat or cold, light or shade, love or hatred, pain or pleasure. I never catch *myself* at any time without a perception, and never can observe anything but the perception . . . . If anyone upon serious and unprejudic'd reflexion, thinks he has a different notion of *himself* I must confess I can reason no longer with him. All I can allow him is, that he may be in the right as well as I, and that we are essentially different in this

> particular. He may, perhaps, perceive
> something simple and continu'd, which he
> calls *himself;* tho' I am certain there is no
> such principle in me.[3]

Herbert Spencer stated clearly the reason why this failure to discover the self was not merely a contingent matter, not something to be attributed to the Scottish philosopher's inattentiveness or sloth. Self is, by definition, the inner perceiver; therefore it cannot be anything that is inwardly perceived.

> If, then, the object perceived is self, what is
> the subject that perceives? Or if it is the true
> self which thinks, what other self can it be that
> is thought of?[4]

For empiricism, the self is an unobjectifiable subject, just as the eye is an invisible organ. But just as the Cartesian ego -- as the locus of intellectual infallibility -- dwindles to nothingness when Cartesian principles are rigorously applied, so too the empiricist self vanishes when subjected to systematic empiricist scrutiny. It is not discoverable by any sense, whether inner or outer; and therefore it is to be rejected as a metaphysical monster.

Very intelligent and sophisticated philosophers of our own age, who are well aware of the internal inconsistencies of Cartesian rationalism and British empiricism, none the less accept the notion of the self, as something different from the human being whose self it is. Let Thomas Nagel be a spokesman for them, in his book *The View from Nowhere*.[5] For Nagel the self is above all a perspectiveless subject of experiences. Ordinary persons see the world from a particular viewpoint; the objective self takes the view from nowhere.

> Essentially I have no particular point of view at all, but apprehend the world as centerless. As it happens, I ordinarily view the world from a certain vantage point, using the eyes, the person, the daily life of TN as a kind of window. But the experiences and the perspective of TN with which I am directly presented are not the point of view of the true self, for the true self has no point of view and includes in its conception of the centerless world TN and his perspective among the contents of that world.[6]

Nagel goes on to make a number of qualifications to this picture: the true self may be something more than this centreless objective subject, and its link with TN may be more than accidental. However, Nagel seems to think also that it would be conceivable that there should be a self which was not identical with, or specially linked to, any person of an ordinary kind. He continues:

> The objective self that I find viewing the world through TN is not unique: each of you has one. Or perhaps I should say each of you is one, for the objective self is not a distinct entity. Each of us, then, in addition to being an ordinary person, is a particular objective self, the subject of a perspectiveless conception of reality.

> We can account for the content of the philosophical thought "I am TN" if we understand the "I" as referring to me qua subject of the impersonal conception of the world which contains TN.[7]

The reader of these passages must ask himself who or what it is that is indicated by the word "I" which occurs in them. Because the author's name is given on the title page as Thomas Nagel, the normal conventions would entitle the reader to assume that the utterer of these "I" sen-

tences is Thomas Nagel. However, the sentences themselves speak of TN as something different, if not distinct, from their
utterer -- something that the utterer makes
use of, and is associated with. We know,
however, that the voice or hand which
transmitted these thoughts to paper was the
voice or hand of Nagel; so we are left with
the eerie feeling that Nagel is being used as
a medium, or ventriloquist's doll, by a spiritual, objective entity speaking through him.
We others, of course, can never be directly
acquainted with Nagel's self; we have to
take Nagel's word for his self's existence, or
at best we have to accept Nagel as speaking
to us on his self's behalf.

At times it seems that there is not
just one but two spirits communicating with
us through Nagel's writing; for when we
read, in the second passage quoted above,
there is an "objective self that I find view-
ing the world through TN" the I who there
speaks is not the objective self that was
speaking a moment ago, but a different I
who comes into contact with the objective
self: we now have a trinity of I, self, and
Nagel. The mental vertigo which all this is
likely to induce in the reader is not
alleviated when we are warned that the self

is not a distinct entity. For it is clear that
Nagel believes that the self is something
different from himself, something that he
is over and above being an ordinary human
being, something that he *has* over and
above having a mind and a body.

What leads Nagel to make these
disturbing and hardly intelligible claims?
There seem to be two main motives. The
first is a desire to make sense of the sentence, "I am Thomas Nagel," in the context
of soliloquy. The sense of "I" must be different from the sense of "Thomas Nagel" if
the sentence is not to be empty. The
second is a feeling that there is something
incongruous in Nagel's having the thought
that Nagel is an insignificant item in the
vast oceans of space and time. Since Nagel
cannot help seeing the world from Nagel's
viewpoint, the conception of a centreless
universe in which Nagel is just a tiny speck
must belong to something other than
Nagel.

Neither of these considerations is
persuasive. There are many contexts in
which the utterance of "I am Thomas
Nagel" has a clear sense: a self-
introduction at a cocktail party; the expression of recovery from amnesia after bad

concussion; the realisation, by a schoolmaster named John Smith, that it is he whom the schoolchildren have been referring to by the nickname "Thomas Nagel." Some of the contexts in which "I am Thomas Nagel" makes sense are soliloquistic ones: Nagel, having written a substandard sentence, may strike it out, saying to himself "I am Thomas Nagel, a philosopher with a reputation to keep up." But the utterance of "I am Thomas Nagel" which is supposed to support the existence of the objective self was not anything like this. It was supposed to be an identity sentence consisting of two referring expressions with different senses, on the model of "The morning star is the evening star." But this is the wrong way to construe sentences of the form "I am N.N." whether in public utterance or in private utterance. And there is no reason to believe that every utterance of "I am N.N." sentences in private will have any sense at all, any more than an utterance of "Come here!" to oneself in the middle of a soliloquy.

In the second place, I find it difficult to understand what is problematic about the supposition that Nagel has the thought that Nagel is an insignificant speck. No doubt this is a matter where each person should speak for himself, but for my part I find no difficulty in believing that Anthony Kenny is a person of no cosmic significance. There were countless ages before I was born, there will be countless ages after I am dead; everything I know is minute compared with all that I do not know, and my hopes and fears are of infinitesimal consequence in the overall scheme of things. To be sure, a great deal of my effort goes into seeking the welfare of this tiny transitory being that is myself; but there is no disproportion here since in the light of eternity my endeavours are just as puny as the purposes they serve. The point is that in all this it is the human being, Anthony Kenny, who is speaking, and it is the human being, Anthony Kenny, who is being spoken about. What is supposed to be incoherent about such self-reference? Why should either the subject or the object of these thoughts be detached from the everyday human being who is doing the thinking of them?

The argument seems to be that human beings must see the world from a viewpoint, and therefore a perspectiveless vision must belong to something other than an ordinary person. But is it true that human beings must see from a viewpoint? If we take the world "see" literally, then it is true that we can only see from a particular point in space, and that we cannot see the organ of our vision. (It is, I believe, only contingently true that I cannot see the back of my neck; but it is necessarily true that an eye cannot, save in a mirror, see itself). But if we take "see" in the broad intellectual sense, to include having beliefs and making judgements about the world, then it does not seem true that we can only see the world from a viewpoint. When we make scientific judgements we are making impersonal, centreless judgements, and the objects of our scientific judgements can perfectly well include ourselves. I can talk about myself, and talk about myself talking about myself, and if I can talk about myself, I can think about myself, either aloud or to myself.

The only reason for denying that it is logically possible to think objectively about oneself seems to be a hangover from the empiricist view of the self. If one thinks of solitary thought on the model of the inner sense, then the contents of the mind are images which are presented to an inner eye in the internal theatre of the imagination. And just as the outer eye cannot see itself, so the inner eye cannot see itself. The true self is therefore thought of as an unviewed viewer. But it is only if we first confuse thought with imagination, and then conceive imagination simply as interior sensation, that we have any reason to deny the possibility of thought about oneself. The very same I, the very same human being, the very same Anthony Kenny is both the thinker of this thought that you are listening to and the topic of this thought that you are listening to.

To Descartes' question "What am I?" my own answer is that I am a human being, a living body of a certain kind. We sometimes speak as if we have bodies, rather than are bodies. But having a body, in this natural sense, is not incompatible with being a body; it does not mean that there is something other than my body which *has* my body. Just as my body has a head, a trunk, two arms, and two legs, but is not something over and above the head, trunk, arms and legs, so I have a body but am not something over and above the body. I also have a soul: that is to say, I have a mind and a will.

To say that I have a mind is to say that I have the capacity to acquire and exercise intellectual abilities of various kinds, such as the mastery of language and the possession of objective information. To say that I have a will is to say that I have the capacity for the free pursuit of goals formulated by the intellect. The mind and the will, as I understand the terms, are capacities. What are they capacities *of*? Of the living human being, the body you see before you.

When I die, my body will cease to be me and I will no longer exist. Some people believe that intellectual and volitional capacities can be exercised apart from the body. I find this difficult to understand. It is true that in the present life there are intellectual and volitional activities which do not involve any bodily activity, such as silent thought and spiritual longings. No doubt even such activities depend on the activity of the brain, but this appears to be a contingent rather than a necessary truth. But it is not a merely contingent fact that the person whose thoughts and longings they are is a visible and tangible body; and I do not for my part find it easy to make sense out of the idea that such activities can take place, and be attributed to individual souls, in the absence of bodies to individuate the souls. For in the sense in which it is undoubtedly true to say that I have a soul, the soul appears to be *my* soul simply and solely because it is the soul of *this* body.

I do not, however, in the present lecture wish to take issue with those who believe in disembodied immortal souls. For nothing I have said so far would necessarily be rejected by those who believe in such souls. In an Aquinas lecture it is appropriate to take St. Thomas as a spokesman for such believers. Aquinas undoubtedly believed that each human being had an immortal soul, which could survive the death of the body and continue to think and will in the period before the eventual resurrection of the body to which he looked forward. None the less, Aquinas did not believe in a self which was distinct from the body, nor did he think that disembodied souls were persons.

This is made clear in a striking passage in his commmentary on the First Epistle to the Corinthians, which was drawn to my attention by Professor Peter Geach.

Commenting on the passage, "If in this life only we have hope in Christ, we are of all men most miserable," St. Thomas wrote:

A human being naturally desires his own salvation; but the soul, since it is part of the body of a human being, is not a whole human being, and my soul is not I; so even if a soul gains salvation in another life, that is not I or any human being.[8]

It is remarkable that St. Thomas says not just that the soul is only a part of a human being, but that it is only part *of the body* of a human being. Commonly he uses "soul" and "body" as correlatives, and often he writes as if soul and body are related to each other as the form and the matter of the Aristotelian hylemorphism. But the formulation which he uses in this passage is in fact the more correct one from the hylemorphic standpoint: the human being is a body which like other mutable bodies is composed of matter and form; the soul, which is the form of the living body, is one part of the body, and the matter is another part of it, using "part" in the very special sense which is appropriate in this context.

What is most clear from the passage is that St. Thomas refuses to identify the disembodied soul, even a beatified disembodied soul, with any self, or ego. According to St. Thomas, what I am, what you are, what everyone else is, is nothing less than a human being. He refuses to identify the individual with the individual's soul, as Descartes was to do. He would not disagree with the theme of this paper that each of us has no self other than himself or herself.

In one very special case, it might be thought, St. Thomas would agree that a human being had a self which was distinct from the soul and body which made him a human being. According to the doctrine of the Incarnation, Jesus Christ is who he is not through the soul and body which constitute his humanity, but because of the divine personality incarnate in him. As Cardinal Newman put it in the hymn "Praise to the Holiest," the special feature of the Incarnation is that

> ... a higher gift than grace
> Should flesh and blood refine
> God's presence and his very Self
> And essence all divine.

But it would be quite wrong to think that the doctrine of the Incarnation involves the thesis that the Divine Self occupied in Jesus the place occupied in the rest of us by the human self. For the philosophers' self was meant to be something central and important to each human being, and someone who lacked such a self would be no real human being, so that if God was to become incarnate as a human he would need to take on a self as well as a soul and a body. If, on the other hand, we accept that the philosophers' self is mythical, then the concept of self cannot be used to mark out a locus for the divine to occupy in the course of the Incarnation. Just as my self is nothing other than myself, so God's Self is just God Himself: it is He, and not any distinct self, human or divine, which according to the Christian doctrine, took on human nature.

For the poets whom I took as the point of depart for this lecture, the self had two essential characteristics: first, it was a secret and private entity, and secondly, it was that part of a human being which was most lasting and essential, by comparison with the superficial and accidental features. Now it is no part of my thesis to deny that

there are elements of our human life that
are private, or that there are elements that
are fundamental. What is wrong with the
doctrine of the self is that it identifies the
fundamental with the private.

Much of my life is private in the
sense that it consists of thoughts and feelings which I keep to myself and do not
express to others. Like most people, I
accompany much of what I do with frag-
mentary inner monologue; each day I have
feelings, suffer moods, entertain fantasies
which I do not trouble to inform other people about. Because these episodes in my
life are not made public, they may seem to
be peculiarly mine, very intimate to myself.
The philosopher's "self" was invented
partly to be a bearer, or observer, of these
secret thoughts and passions. Self-
knowledge, according to the philosophy of
the self, is the monitoring of this inward
life.

It would be absurd, however, to
claim that my private imaginings constitute
that which, in the words of the Dictionary,
is "really and intrinsically me in
contradistinction to what is adventitious."
To be sure, someone who had access to all
my private imaginings would know a little

more about me than someone who was privy only to my public utterances: she would learn, for instance, about various remarks which had come into my mind to make, but which I had suppressed for reasons of prudence or politeness. But remarks which occur and are not even made are at least as adventitious items in my life as remarks which are actually made. Indeed, the fact that I suppressed certain remarks is often a more important fact about me than the fact that they came into my mind in the first place.

The really important questions about oneself, about what kind of person one fundamentally is, are not questions which can be settled by introspection. "Do I really love her?" "Am I the kind of person that would betray a friend to death to save my life?" "Will I regret, in five years time, that I changed my job in mid-life?" "Am I getting more and more vain as I grow older?" These, and countless other questions of the same kind, are questions which receive their definitive answer not in private colloquy with oneself in the imagination, but in the testing conditions of life in the real and public world. A close friend or spouse may well be able to conjecture in advance with greater perspicacity than I the answers they will eventually receive.

As with self-knowledge, so with self-love. When I am selfish, the good which I am pursuing is the good of the human being, Anthony Kenny, not the good of some inner entity in the theatre of the imagination. Those who pursue pleasure and power for themselves are seeking not pleasure and power in the inner world of the imagination, but in the public world of flesh and blood. Unselfishness, too, is measured not by interior acts of secret renunciation, but by the willingness to put first the interests of other human beings in the public world. The self that is cosseted or disciplined is not the inner observer of the mental theatre, nor the centreless subject of objectivity: it is the human being with all the parts and passions of a man.

The concept of the self which I have been attacking is that which urges us to look within for that which is most fundamental in ourselves. This is a philosophical notion which, as I have illustrated, has had a great influence outside philosophy as well. But it would be wrong to think that it is the only philosophical notion of the self.

There is a quite different concept which regards the self as what is expressed by the uniquely characteristic actions of the individual. In this sense, it is not only conscious beings which have selves. This notion of self, too, has deep philosophical roots, but connected to a philosophy different from those which have been considered here. It would itself be a topic for a whole lecture. On this occasion I merely mention it to distinguish it from the kind of self which provided the topic today. I can end by quoting verses which express this different concept: for this notion of self too has found magisterial poetic expression -- in the words of Gerard Manley Hopkins.

As kingfishers catch fire, dragonflies draw flame
    As tumbled over rim in roundy wells
    Stones ring; like each tucked string tells,
       each hung bell's
Bow swung finds tongue to fling out broad its name;
    Each mortal thing does one thing and the same:
    Deals out that being indoors each one dwells;
    Selves -- goes its self; myself it speaks and spells
Crying *what I do is me: for that I came.*

Balliol. 12-20-87

ENDNOTES

1. Cf. A. Kenny, "A Self out of Season," in *Good Talk*, ed. Derwent May (London: Gollancz, 1968), p. 200.

2. Cf. G. E. M. Anscombe, "The First Person," in *Mind and Language*, ed. S. Guttenplan (Oxford: Clarendon Press, 1975), pp. 45-66, and my "The First Person," in *The Legacy of Wittgenstein* (Oxford: Blackwell, 1984), pp. 77-87.

3. See the *Treatise of Human Nature*, ed. Selby-Bigge, Oxford, 1928, p. 252.

4. See *First Principles* 1.III 20.

5. New York: Oxford University Press, 1986.

6. See *The View from Nowhere*, p. 61.

7. Ibid., p. 64.

8. "Constat quod homo naturaliter desiderat salutem sui ipsius, anima autem cum sit pars corporis hominis, non est totus homo, et anima mea non est ego; unde licet anima consequatur salutem in alia vita, non tamen ego vel quilibet homo." In *I ad Corinthios* XV, l. 11, ed. Cai, 924.

140, 912

The Aquinas Lectures
Published by the Marquette University Press
Milwaukee, Wisconsin 53233
United States of America

= =

#1 **St. Thomas and the Life of Learning.** John F. McCormick, S.J. (1937). ISBN 0-87462-101-1

#2 **St. Thomas and the Gentiles.** Mortimer J. Adler (1938). ISBN 0-87462-102-X

#3 **St. Thomas and the Greeks.** Anton C. Pegis (1939). ISBN 0-87462-103-8

#4 **The Nature and Functions of Authority.** Yves Simon (1940). ISBN 0-87462-104-6

#5 **St. Thomas and Analogy.** Gerald B. Phelan (1941). ISBN 0-87462-105-4

#6 **St. Thomas and the Problem of Evil.** Jacques Maritain (1942). ISBN 0-87462-106-2

Uniform format, cover, and binding.

Copies of this Aquinas Lecture and the others in the series are obtainable from:

Marquette University Press
Marquette University
Milwaukee, Wisconsin 53233, U.S.A.

Publishers of:

*Medieval Philosophical Texts in Translation
*Pere Marquette Theology Lectures
*St. Thomas Aquinas Lectures